BULLDOGS

by Martha E. H. Rustad

AMICUS HIGH INTEREST • AMICUS INK

Amicus High Interest and Amicus Ink are imprints of Amicus
P.O. Box 1329, Mankato, MN 56002
www.amicuspublishing.us

Library of Congress Cataloging-in-Publication Data
Names: Rustad, Martha E. H. (Martha Elizabeth Hillman), 1975- author.
Title: Bulldogs / by Martha E. H. Rustad.
Description: Mankato, Minnesota : Amicus High Interest, Amicus Ink,
  [2018] | Series: Favorite dog breeds | Audience: K to grade 3. | Includes
  bibliographical references and index.
Identifiers: LCCN 2016033324| ISBN 9781681511269 (library binding) |
  ISBN 9781681521572 (pbk.) | ISBN 9781681512167 (ebook)
Subjects: LCSH: Bulldog--Juvenile literature. | Dog breeds--Juvenile
  literature.
Classification: LCC SF429.B85 R87 2018 | DDC 636.72--dc23
LC record available at https://lccn.loc.gov/2016033324

Photo Credits: Eric Isselee/shutterstock cover, 2, 10; ihorga/iStock 5;
Duncan, P. Martin/WikiCommons 6; otsphoto/shutterstock 8-9; Juan
Sebastian Avila/shutterstock 12-13; Ammit Jack/shutterstock 14-15; John
McAllister/123rf 17; WilleeCole Photography/shutterstock 18-19; Tanya
Constantine/Alamy 20-21; Isselee/Dreamstime 22

Editor: Wendy Dieker
Designer: Tracy Myers
Photo Researcher: Holly Young

Printed in the United States of America

HC 10 9 8 7 6 5 4 3 2 1
PB 10 9 8 7 6 5 4 3 2 1

TABLE OF CONTENTS

SLEEPY DOG

Snore! A dog rolls over. The eyes in his wrinkled face are shut. He snorts. He drools. Ding-dong! He wakes up. His head shakes. Drool flies! Bulldogs are noisy and messy.

Furry Fact
Bulldogs nap often. But they need walks every day to stay healthy.

BULL DOG.

BULL FIGHTERS

The bulldog breed began in England. The dogs once worked on farms. Owners **trained** them to fight with bulls. Today, people know bulldogs as friendly pets.

SQUARE BODY

A bulldog's body is strong and wide. They are medium sized. But they weigh a lot. Their front legs are shorter than their back legs. This makes them waddle. These dogs do not run fast.

Furry Fact
Some bulldogs have short, straight tails. Others have curly tails.

BIG HEAD

A bulldog has a big head. Its lower teeth stick out. Its strong jaws can grip toys. A bulldog's tongue hangs out. Its nose is short and squished.

SNORTING DOG

With such a short nose, bulldogs can have breathing problems. Bulldogs breathe through their mouths. They snore and snort.

Furry Fact
The extra air bulldogs breathe in has to get out somehow. Bulldogs pass a lot of gas. Stinky!

WRINKLY SKIN

Bulldogs have loose skin. Wrinkles cover their faces and bodies. Owners must clean in the wrinkles. The bulldog's **coat** can be many colors. It can be brown, black, or white.

PUPPIES

Newborn bulldogs are helpless. They are born with their eyes closed. Pet owners watch the puppies closely. They help the puppies drink their mother's milk.

Furry Fact
Bulldog puppies grow quickly. They double in size after a month.

TRAINING

Bulldogs can be **stubborn**. These dogs are not always easy to train. They like treats as rewards. Owners keep training sessions short.

FRIENDLY BULLY

Bulldogs look like tough fighters. But they are sweet dogs. They are patient with kids. They like to play with their families.

Furry Fact
Lots of schools have a bulldog for a mascot. They look so strong and fierce.

HOW DO YOU KNOW IT'S A BULLDOG?

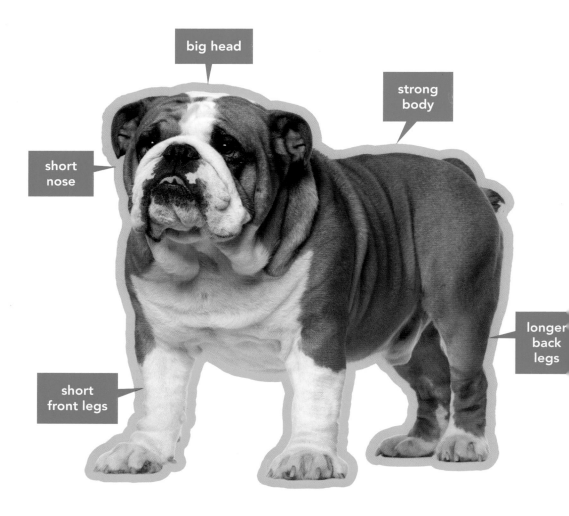

big head

strong body

short nose

longer back legs

short front legs

WORDS TO KNOW

coat – the fur of a dog

mascot – an animal that stands for a group or sports team; people think mascots bring good luck

stubborn – refusing to obey or change a way of doing something

train – to teach how to behave

LEARN MORE

Books

Bozzo, Linda. *I Like Bulldogs!* New York: Enslow, 2017.

Riggs, Kate. *Bulldogs.* Mankato, Minn.: Creative Education, 2016.

Schuh, Mari. *Bulldogs.* Minneapolis: Bellwether Media, 2016.

Websites

American Kennel Club: The Bulldog
http://www.akc.org/dog-breeds/bulldog/

Bulldog Breed
http://dogtime.com/dog-breeds/bulldog

Bulldog Personality
https://www.rover.com/blog/english-bulldogs-personality/

INDEX